WHAT'S INSIDE
Headphones?

Published by The Child's World®
1980 Lookout Drive • Mankato, MN 56003-1705
800-599-READ • www.childsworld.com

Photographs ©: Rick Orndorf, cover (headphones), 1 (headphones), 4, 7, 8 (speaker), 9 (top), 9 (bottom), 10, 11, 13 (top), 13 (bottom left), 13 (bottom right), 14 (jack), 15 (speaker), 17, 18 (headphones), 21, 24; Rob Cartorres/Shutterstock Images, cover (jack), 1 (jack), 6 (jack), 8 (jack), 23; Sommart Sombutwanitkul/Shutterstock Images, cover (speaker), 1 (speaker), 6 (speaker), 16, 20 (speaker), 22; Shutterstock Images, 2, 3 (plug), 3 (circuit board), 5 (glasses), 19; Praiwun Thungsarn/ Shutterstock Images, 3 (screwdriver), 5 (screwdriver), 12, 20 (screwdriver); Shyripa Alexandr/ Shutterstock Images, 5 (gloves); Krisana Antharith/Shutterstock Images, 14 (wire), 15 (wire), 18 (wire)

ISBN 9781503832367
LCCN 2018963099

Printed in the United States of America
PA02419

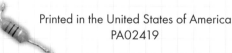

About the Author

Arnold Ringstad lives in Minnesota.

He listens to music on headphones every day.

Contents

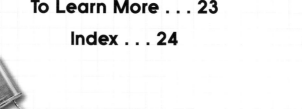

Materials and Safety

Materials

- ☐ Headphones
- ☐ Safety glasses
- ☐ Standard screwdriver
- ☐ Work gloves

Safety

- Make sure the headphones are not plugged in before taking them apart.

- Be careful when handling sharp objects, such as screwdrivers.

- Wear work gloves to protect your hands from sharp edges.

- Wear safety glasses in case pieces snap off.

Headphones

Work gloves

Standard screwdriver

Safety glasses

Inside Headphones

People love listening to music. But sometimes they don't want to bother others around them. They can use headphones to enjoy music alone. How do headphones work? What's inside?

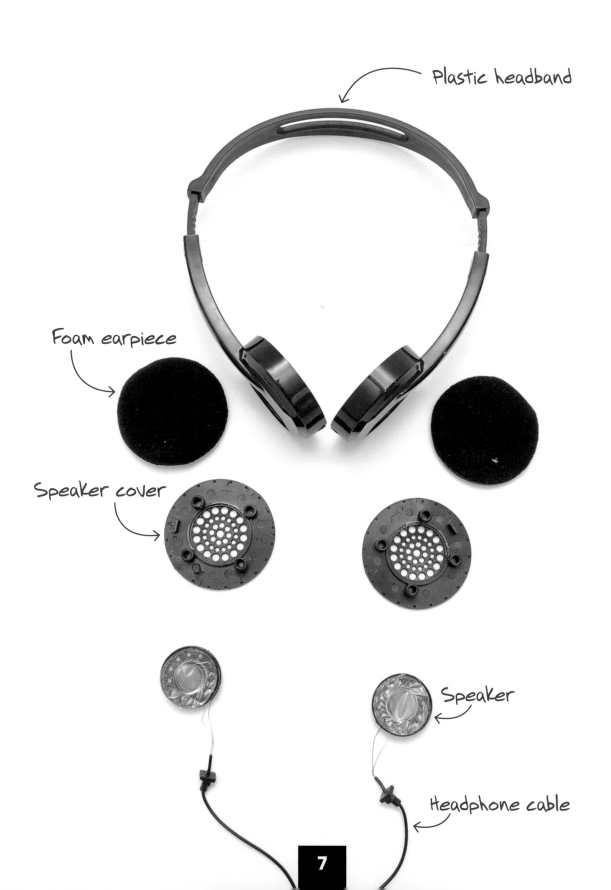

Plastic headband

Foam earpiece

Speaker cover

Speaker

Headphone cable

The Headband

The largest part of the headphones is the headband. It is made of hard plastic. A middle piece connects to the two sides. Notches in the plastic let people make the sides longer or shorter. This lets them adjust the headphones to their head size.

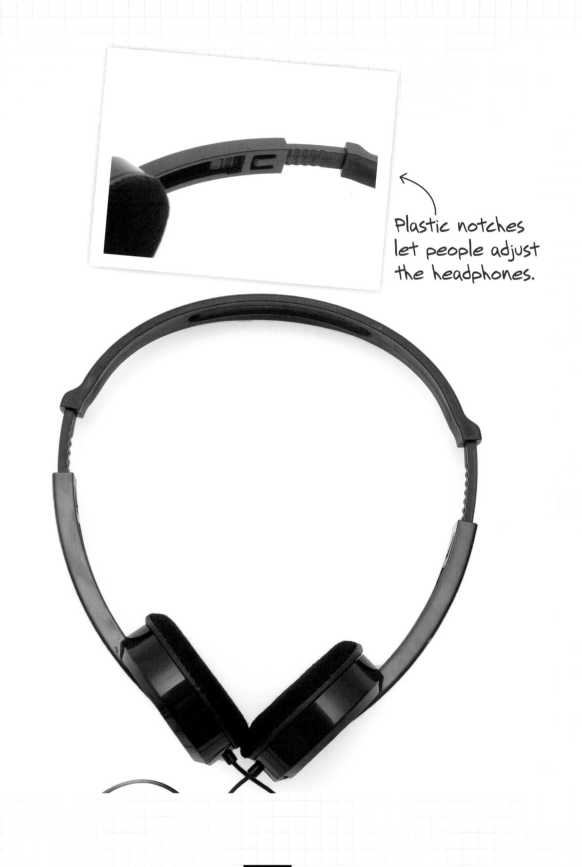

Plastic notches
let people adjust
the headphones.

Earpieces

Each side has a speaker on the end. The speakers are covered by hard plastic and a foam earpiece. The foam sits between the hard plastic and the user's ear. This makes the headphones more comfortable to wear. Pull the earpiece off to reveal the plastic below.

Foam earpiece

Removing the Speaker Cover

Use a standard screwdriver to pull the front of the speaker cover away. Then turn the speaker cover over. The speaker itself is glued into place in the cover. Carefully remove it. You can use the screwdriver to gently pull it away.

Safety Note

Screwdrivers are sharp, so be careful when pulling the headphones open.

The speaker
cover can
be pulled
away from
the rest of
the headphones.

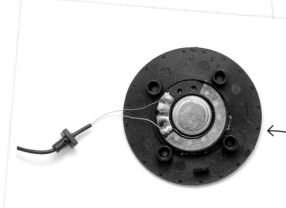

The speaker
is glued onto
the cover.

Receiving Signals

Each speaker has two wires going into it. These come from an **audio** cable. The other end of the cable plugs into an audio **jack**.

The audio cable fits into many kinds of devices.

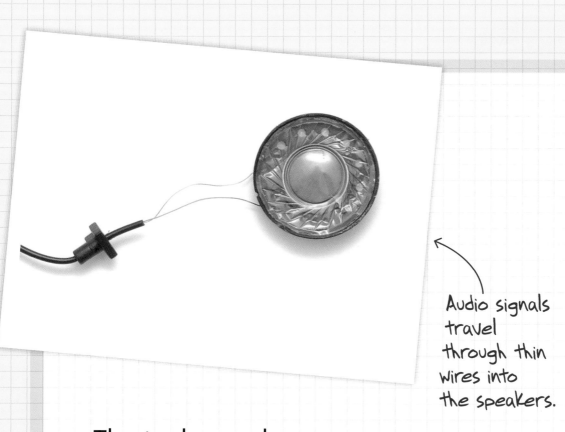

Audio signals travel through thin wires into the speakers.

The jack may be on a computer, a phone, or anything else that plays music. The device creates electrical signals. It sends them through the audio cable to the speakers.

Magnets

Electrical signals travel into the speaker. They enter a metal coil. The coil is an **electromagnet**. It becomes magnetic when electricity goes through it. The signals rapidly make the coil's magnetism stronger or weaker. The coil pushes against a large magnet. The magnet makes the coil **vibrate** quickly.

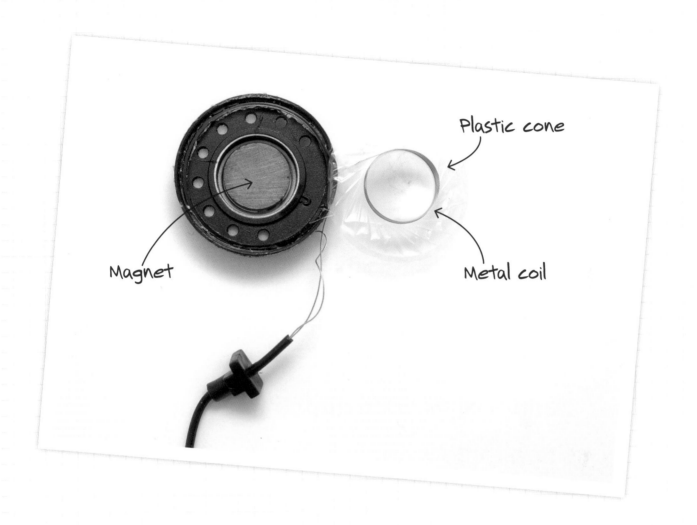

Plastic cone

Magnet

Metal coil

As the coil vibrates back and forth, it pushes a thin plastic cone along with it.

Making Sound

The plastic cone's motion creates waves of air pressure. We hear this air pressure as sound. The headphones have turned electrical signals into music!

Reusing Headphones

We've taken apart headphones and learned what's inside. Now what? Here are some ideas for how to reuse the parts of headphones. Can you think of any more?

- **Fridge Magnet**: The speakers have magnets inside. Try using them as fridge magnets! How strong are they compared to other fridge magnets?

- **Necklace**: Use the speakers and audio cables to make a necklace. Can you use the magnets as a clasp to hold the necklace together?

Glossary

audio (AH-dee-oh): Audio is recorded sound or music. An audio cable carries the sound from a device to the headphones.

electromagnet (i-lek-troh-MAG-nit): An electromagnet is a magnet that pulls things toward it when only electricity flows through it. Inside the speaker, the coil is an electromagnet.

jack (JAK): A jack is a place where cords can plug in to send or receive signals. Many devices have a jack where headphones can be plugged in.

vibrate (VYE-brate): When something is caused to vibrate, it shakes back and forth quickly. Inside the speaker, magnetism makes the coil vibrate.

To Learn More

IN THE LIBRARY

Connors, Kathleen. *Sound*. New York, NY:
Gareth Stevens Publishing, 2019.

Hall, Pamela. *Discover Sound*. Mankato,
MN: The Child's World, 2015.

Holzweiss, Kristina. *Amazing Makerspace DIY with
Electricity*. New York, NY: Scholastic, 2018.

ON THE WEB

Visit our website for links about taking apart
headphones: **childsworld.com/links**

Note to Parents, Teachers, and Librarians: We routinely verify our Web links to make sure they
are safe and active sites. So encourage your readers to check them out!

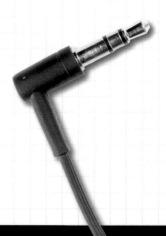

Index